SWIMMING
WITH
SAURS

3D
DINOSAUR
DISCOVERY™

by
**Kathleen
Kranking**

with
**Matthew T.
Carrano,** Ph.D.
Consultant

Mosasaur mouth

Scholastic Inc.

New York   Toronto   London   Auckland   Sydney
Mexico City   New Delhi   Hong Kong   Buenos Aires

ISBN 0-439-83875-4

Designers: Bob Budiansky and Lee Kaplan.

Cover illustration: *Mosasaurus* © Jaime Chirinos.

Title page photo: (Mosasaur mouth) © Kris Kripchak.

Back cover illustration: Ginsu shark and mosasaur © Julius Csotonyi.

All Ty the *Tyrannosaurus rex* illustrations by Ed Shems.

All 3-D conversions by Pinsharp 3D Graphics.

Interior Photo and Illustration Credits:
Pages 4–5: *Ophthalmosaurus*, *Cryptoclidus*, and *Liopleurodon* © Todd Marshall.
Pages 6–7: *Dunkleosteus* © Jaime Chirinos.
Pages 8–9: *Morenosaurus* © Todd Marshall.
Page 10: *Woolungasaurus* © Todd Marshall; (Loch Ness) © Adrian T Jones/Shutterstock.com.
Page 11: *Kronosaurus* © Todd Marshall.
Pages 12–13: *Liopleurodon* and young © Stephen Missal; (plesiosaur exhibit) © Kris Kripchak.
Pages 14–15: *Tylosaurus* © Karl Huber; (mosasaur mouth) © Kris Kripchak.
Page 16: *Mosasaurus* © Jaime Chirinos.
Page 17: *Ichthyosaurus* © Julius Csotonyi.
Pages 18–19: *Shonisaurus* and *Californosaurus* © Todd Marshall; (*Ichthyosaurus* skeleton) © Jonathan Blair/Corbis.
Pages 20–21: All marine reptile illustrations © John Bindon; (planet Earth) R. Stockli/ Robert Simmon/NASA GFC/MODIS.
Page 22: *Megalodon* © Todd Marshall.
Page 23: Ginsu shark and mosasaur © Julius Csotonyi.
Page 24: *Xiphactinus* © Stephen Missal; (*Xiphactinus* skeleton) © Kris Kripchak.
Page 25: *Protosphyraena* © Stephen Missal; *Enchodus* © Jaime Chirinos.
Pages 26–27: *Archelon* © Karl Huber; (*Protostega* skeleton) © Kris Kripchak; (turtle hatchling) © Kevin Schafer/Corbis.
Page 28: Crinoids and blastoids © Todd Marshall.
Page 29: (Fossil ammonites) © Jason Vandehey/Shutterstock.com; *Tusoteuthis* © Stephen Missal.
Page 30: (Robin O'Keefe) © Eric Duneman.
Page 31: *Henodus* © Stephen Missal.
Page 32: Ammonite © Todd Marshall.

12 11 10 9 8 7 6 5 4 3 2   6 7 8 9 10 11/0

Printed in the U.S.A.

First Scholastic printing, July 2006

TABLE OF CONTENTS

Ty
Tyrannosaurus rex
(tie-RAN-oh-SOR-uhss
RECKS)

Welcome back! It's me, your friend Ty. And it's time for another **3-D Dinosaur Discovery** adventure. We've already met some of the biggest monsters to live on land—dinosaurs! Now we'll meet some monsters of the sea: **marine (muh-REEN) reptiles**. Some of these animals make today's ocean giants look like guppies! Did you know that:

◆ Some marine reptiles had necks that were longer than their whole bodies?

◆ There were marine reptiles with eyes as big as dinner plates?

◆ Parts of the United States used to be underwater?

Dino Dictionary
A *marine* animal lives in the ocean.

Ophthalmosaurus
(op-THAL-moh-SOR-uhss)

WITH SAURS!

Cryptoclidus
(KRIP-toe-CLIDE-duhss)

And we'll go fishing for answers to lots of questions, like:

◆ Were marine reptiles deep divers?

◆ Were there sharks in the Mesozoic?

◆ Why did some marine reptiles eat rocks for breakfast?

As we're swimming along, be sure to put on your **3-D glasses** when you see this icon to see these monsters pop off the page.

Are you ready to begin an adventure? Turn the page and dive right in!

Liopleurodon
(LIE-oh-PLUR-oh-don)

Splash! Here we are in the prehistoric ocean! As you swim along, you'll see that in some ways, it's a lot like today's ocean. It's wet and salty. And some of the animals look familiar, like fish, turtles, and jellyfish.

But in the Mesozoic Era, the ocean was different from today's ocean in some important ways. For one thing, the water was warmer, and there weren't any icy parts around the North and South Poles. And back in the Mesozoic, the ocean covered lots of places where there's dry land today. In fact, the whole middle of the United States was underwater!

But the biggest difference between the Mesozoic ocean and today's ocean is that no matter where we swim, we won't see any whales or other large mammals. Instead, we'd see BIG reptiles that are super-fierce **predators** (PRED-uh-turs). Yikes!

I'll need some swimming lessons!

Dunkleosteus (DUNK-kull-OSS-tee-uhss), **a Paleozoic** (PAIL-lee-oh-ZOE-ik) **fish.**

Dino 🦕 Dictionary

A *predator* hunts and kills other animals for food. The animals a predator kills and eats are its *prey*.

Marine reptiles were the largest ocean predators in the Mesozoic. Some of these super-scary reptiles were much bigger and more dangerous than any meat-eating dinosaur on land. We're going to check out some of these animals. Grab your 3-D glasses, and let's go!

DINO DATA

Remember, dinosaurs lived on land, while marine reptiles lived mainly in water. Marine reptiles also had paddles or flippers, which no dino had. So although both groups of animals were reptiles, marine reptiles were definitely not dinosaurs!

Paddle right up and meet the **plesiosaurs** (PLEE-zee-oh-sors)! Plesiosaurs lived from the end of the Triassic all the way through the Cretaceous. They included some of the biggest predators that ever lived! Check out these pages to learn more about these underwater giants.

It's All in the Neck: Elasmosaurs

There were two main kinds of plesiosaurs and it was pretty easy to tell them apart. It was all in the neck! Let's start with the long-necked **elasmosaurs** (eh-LAZZ-moh-sors).

Even though some elasmosaurs were giants, they couldn't eat very large prey because **their heads and mouths were so small**. Scientists think that the biggest elasmosaurs didn't eat anything longer than a skateboard.

An elasmosaur's neck was its most famous feature. The biggest elasmosaurs had more than 70 **vertebrae** (VUR-tuh-bray) in their necks. That's 10 times more bones than you have in your neck!

Dino Dictionary

Vertebrae are bones that make up the neck and spine.

Elasmosaurs, like all marine reptiles, **breathed air**. They probably came to the ocean's surface to take a deep breath, and then held it in while swimming underwater.

All plesiosaurs had **four stiff paddles**. Inside each paddle were five very long fingers made up of 24 or more bones. Since humans only have three bones in each of their fingers, that's a lot! Most scientists think that plesiosaurs swam by flapping their paddles like wings and "flying" through the water like penguins do today.

Plesiosaurs

Morenosaurus
(more-RAY-noh-SOR-uhss)

DINO DATA

Early paleontologists saw that the bones of the first plesiosaur fossil looked a lot like a lizard's... except for those flippers! So they named it *plesiosaur*, which means "near lizard."

Woolungasaurus
(woo-LUNG-guh-SOR-uhss)

Slow 'n' Sneaky

Because of their long necks, elasmosaurs were probably slow swimmers. They couldn't catch prey like fish and squid by chasing after it. Instead, they had to be sneaky. An elasmosaur probably swam under a school of fish, moving its small head slowly toward them while hiding its body way below. Then it would use its long, slender teeth to chomp up a fish by surprise!

Rocks for Breakfast

Scientists have found elasmosaurs with hundreds of rocks in their stomachs. That's right, rocks! These rocks, which could be as big as a softball, are called **gastroliths** (GAS-troh-liths). No one knows for sure why elasmosaurs swallowed them. The rocks might have helped elasmosaurs digest their food, since they couldn't chew too well with their teeth. Or, gastroliths might have helped these animals stay underwater, instead of floating up while they were swimming.

Now that's a heavy meal!

A MONSTER MYTH

Some people say they've seen a long-necked sea creature in Loch Ness, a lake in Scotland. And some people even think that the monster, nicknamed "Nessie," might be a plesiosaur. But plesiosaurs went extinct millions of years ago—way before Loch Ness was even formed!

Loch Ness in Scotland

Rough 'n' Tough: Pliosaurs

Now let's check out the other group of plesiosaurs: **pliosaurs** (PLY-oh-sors). They were a lot different from their slow, noodle-necked cousins. Check out the picture below and see!

While elasmosaurs had long necks and small heads, pliosaurs had **strong, short necks and long, crocodile-like heads**.

Just like all marine reptiles, **pliosaurs breathed air**—they didn't have gills like fish do.

Kronosaurus
(KROH-noh-SOR-uhss)

Pliosaurs had **big heads and mouths** with **thick teeth** for tearing at meat.

Like elasmosaurs, pliosaurs also had **four stiff paddles** which they used to swim through the water.

Q: What do you call a polite marine reptile?

A: A *please*-siosaur!

Short But Speedy

Since their necks were shorter, pliosaurs probably swam faster than elasmosaurs. Swimming faster meant that pliosaurs could chase down a meal if it tried to escape. With bigger heads up to 6–8 feet (2–2½ m) long, pliosaurs could prey on large fish and often ate other marine reptiles, including elasmosaurs!

Liopleurodon and young

DINO DATA

Scientists think that plesiosaurs flapped their paddles like they were trying to row a boat when they were swimming. And since their paddles were stiff, they stuck out like airplane wings, even when a plesiosaur was resting.

Water Babies

Scientists first thought that plesiosaurs hatched from eggs, like most reptiles do today. Now most scientists think that it would've been too hard for these enormous reptiles to leave the water since their paddles were too stiff to use on land. Instead, scientists think that plesiosaurs had **live births**, like dogs, cats, and humans do. But unlike these animals, plesiosaurs probably made eggs with shells inside their bodies and kept them there until they hatched.

Dino Dictionary

In *live birth*, an animal's babies grow inside the mother's body first, and then are born alive.

DINO DATA

In 1987, scientists found a plesiosaur fossil with the bones of a baby plesiosaur inside of it. If other plesiosaurs were found with babies inside them, that would help prove that plesiosaurs did have live births. But so far, this is the only one!

A plesiosaur exhibit

MONSTER MOUTHS:

Let's check out the scariest sea monster of the Late Cretaceous. It's a **mosasaur** (MOE-suh-SOR). These reptiles were the top predators in the ocean at the same time that *T. rex* was the top predator on land.

Check out this mosasaur to learn more about these prehistoric monsters!

Hey, we were neighbors!

Mosasaurs had very **long tails**, which were flattened at the end to work like a fifth paddle. Mosasaurs had a different way of swimming from plesiosaurs, too (see page 8). They swung their tails quickly from side to side, wiggled their bodies to push them forward, and used their side paddles to change direction.

Mosasaurs' paddles had **five fingers**, with fewer bones than plesiosaurs. Unlike plesiosaurs, mosasaurs' paddles were **flexible** and probably could be folded against their bodies.

Though mosasaurs could zip for short distances, they couldn't swim at high speeds for a long time to chase prey. Instead, scientists think that these reptiles **hid and surprised their prey**, and then snapped it up fast! Mosasaurs weren't picky eaters, either. Scientists have found their tooth marks on all kinds of fossils. They chowed down on fish, squid, plesiosaurs, and even other mosasaurs.

Mosasaurs

Do you think that this mosasaur looks like a big, swimming lizard? It's not just looks! Mosasaurs are actually related to today's **monitor lizards** and **modern snakes**.

Tylosaurus (TIE-loh-SOR-uhss)

There's a reason mosasaurs were such monster munchers. Unlike elasmosaurs, which had small heads (see page 8), mosasaurs had **big heads** with mouths to match. On each side of a mosasaur's lower jaw was a special joint. These joints let a mosasaur open its mouth extra wide to fit in a super-sized snack.

Mosasaurs also had **special teeth on the roof of their mouths** to help them munch. These "holding" teeth hooked into prey and held it in place while the mosasaur ate. Each time the mosasaur flexed its jaws and swallowed more of its meal, these teeth gripped the prey so it wouldn't fall out.

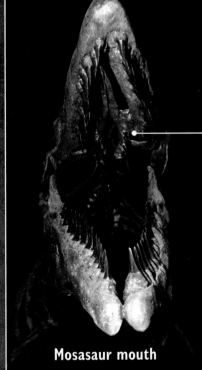

Mosasaur mouth

DINO DATA

The first mosasaur fossil was found in the Netherlands about 225 years ago—50 years before the discovery of dinos! Scientists also find more mosasaurs than any other marine reptile. In some places, they've found 10 times more mosasaur fossils than plesiosaur fossils!

Mosasaurs lived in shallow waters near the coast and probably weren't deep divers. Since mosasaurs look a lot like modern-day lizards, scientists think that early mosasaurs might have been able to live both on land and in water. But by the end of the Cretaceous, mosasaurs were definitely only monsters of the sea.

Mosasaurus
(MOE-suh-SOR-uhss)

Baby Talk

Usually a modern-day reptile mom lays lots and lots of eggs and then leaves them all by themselves. But scientists think that mosasaurs gave birth to a few live young instead of laying eggs. Mosasaur babies might have stayed with their moms until they were big enough to take care of themselves. Or they might have just swum off right away, like sea turtle babies do today.

SOMETHING FISHY:
Ichthyosaurs

Ichthyosaurs (ICK-thee-oh-SORS) were one of the first marine reptiles to make a splash in the Mesozoic ocean. They appeared about 250 million years ago, during the Triassic, before dinosaurs even lived on land. Check out the picture below to learn more about these prehistoric creatures!

From studying fossil skin **impressions** (im-PRESH-shuns) of ichthyosaurs, scientists have figured out that these reptiles had fins on their backs called **dorsal** (DOOR-suhl) **fins**. These fins helped the animal keep balanced while it swam underwater.

Dino Dictionary

An *impression* is a shape, pattern, or other mark made when something is pressed into a soft surface, like sand or mud.

Ichthyosaurus
(ICK-thee-oh-SOR-uhss)

Ichthyosaurs had **crescent-shaped tails**. They swam by swishing their tails side to side, the way most fish do.

Although they had a fishy body shape, ichthyosaurs **breathed air**.

Ichthyosaurs had **two stiff paddles** on the sides of their bodies. Inside each paddle were fingers with lots of short, wide bones that made them look like corncobs!

On the Move

Ichthyosaurs were built for speedy swimming. They probably hunted in the open ocean, grabbing prey with their long, toothy snouts. Fossils found in the stomachs of ichthyosaurs show that they ate mostly squid and some fish, but some of the biggest ones might have eaten other marine reptiles, too. And when it came to finding prey, scientists think that some ichthyosaurs were deep divers.

What Big Eye Rings You Have

It gets pretty dark in the deep ocean, but that wasn't a problem for ichthyosaurs! Ichthyosaurs had huge eyes to help them see in the dark. By looking at the

Shonisaurus (SHO-nee-SOR-uhss) **and a pack of** *Californosaurus* (kal-lee-FORN-oh-SOR-uhss).

sclerotic (skluh-ROT-tik) **rings** inside the skulls of fossil ichthyosaurs, scientists can tell how big their eyes were—and guess how well they could see. One ichthyosaur, *Ophthalmosaurus*, had some especially big peepers. *Ophthalmosaurus* was as long as two adult humans, but its eyes were about 10 inches (25 cm) wide—the size of dinner plates!

Strange Backbones

Besides their giant eyes, ichthyosaurs had another unusual feature—their backbones. While most reptiles have vertebrae shaped like soda cans, ichthyosaurs had vertebrae like big hockey pucks. This might have to do with ichthyosaurs' fishy shape, since other thick-bodied fish have this kind of vertebrae, too.

Let 'Em Loose

Paleontologists know for sure that ichthyosaurs gave birth to live young. They've found lots of fossils that show baby ichthyosaurs inside their moms' bodies. They've even found fossils that show ichthyosaurs giving birth! But scientists think that ichthyosaur moms let their babies swim off to do their own thing as soon as they were born.

JUNIOR FOSSIL HUNTER

Ichthyosaurus fossil

You don't have to be a grown-up to discover a brand-new marine reptile. That's what happened to a 12-year-old girl named Mary Anning back in 1811. Mary's family dug out and sold Jurassic fossils from cliffs near their home in Great Britain. One day, Mary began digging out a skull that her brother had noticed in the cliffs. It was a new kind of ichthyosaur called *Ichthyosaurus*. Although fossils of other ichthyosaurs had been found, this was the first complete skeleton ever discovered. And maybe marine reptiles were Mary's lucky charm! She also discovered the skeleton of the first plesiosaur in 1820.

The Mesozoic Era is known as "The Age of Reptiles," because reptiles ruled—dinos on land and marine reptiles in the ocean. This time line shows when each of the marine reptiles we've met appeared, and how long they hung around.

The Triassic Period

(about 252–200 million years ago)

The first marine reptiles to appear were the **ichthyosaurs**, which came swimming into the Mesozoic ocean about 250 million years ago, during the Early Triassic. The earliest ichthyosaurs looked like lizards, but by the Middle Triassic, they had become fish-shaped and there were many different kinds. By the Late Triassic, some ichthyosaurs had become gigantic. They were the biggest and fastest predators around. Ichthyosaurs went extinct by the Late Cretaceous—before dinos and some other reptiles died out.

The Jurassic Period

(about 200–146 million years ago)

Plesiosaurs appeared at the end of the Triassic. At that time, most were only about 10–12 feet long (3–4 m). But by the second half of the Jurassic, they had become monster-sized like *Liopleurodon*, which was 33 feet (10 m) long and weighed 4–5 tons! Pliosaurs, the faster of the two types of plesiosaurs, replaced ichthyosaurs as the top predators in the ocean during the Late Jurassic.

Ichthyosaurus

Elasmosaurus (eh-LAZZ-moh-SOR-uhss)

WATER WHEN?

Reptiles really made a splash in the Mesozoic!

The Cretaceous Period

▲

(about 146–65 million years ago)

Mosasaurs appeared in the Late Cretaceous. Many types of ichthyosaurs had already become extinct by this time, and shortly after the mosasaurs appeared, all the ichthyosaurs were gone. Mosasaurs were the top predators of their time, eating plesiosaurs and almost anything else.

Mosasaurus

WHERE'D THEY GO?

So what happened to all the sea monsters? Scientists think that whatever wiped out the dinosaurs at the end of the Cretaceous also hit the large marine reptiles that were left in the Mesozoic ocean. Some scientists think that a big meteor hit the Earth and kicked up enough dust to block out the sun. With no sunlight to help plants grow, finding food wasn't easy for both plant-eaters and predators. Other scientists think that changes in the weather at the end of the Cretaceous might have made it hard for big marine reptiles to survive, too.

Hey, don't get out of the water just yet! It's time to check out some other critters that shared the seas with the marine reptiles you've met so far. Flip through these pages and get to know the neighbors.

Move Over, Jaws!

If you were swimming in the Mesozoic ocean and saw something that looked like a great white shark, there'd be good news and bad news. The good news is that it couldn't be a great white. That shark didn't live in the Mesozoic. The bad news is that other sharks even bigger and more dangerous did! Check out these pages to see how sharks took a bite out of the Mesozoic!

I think I'll stick to dry land!

OLDER
THAN
DINOSAURS

The very first sharks appeared in the Paleozoic Era, about 300 million years before the Mesozoic. And they were a weird-looking group—one had a dorsal fin that was shaped like an ironing board and another had a toothy jaw that twirled into a spiral. But lots of modern-day sharks have been around since the Cretaceous, including sand sharks, goblin sharks, and nurse sharks.

Megalodon (MEG-uh-loh-don), a **Cenozoic** (SEN-oh-ZOE-ik) **shark.**

Keep on Chompin'

Fossil mosasaur bones have been found with bite marks from prehistoric sharks. Some bones even have teeth that broke off as a shark chowed down. Some scientists think that the mosasaurs were dead when the sharks attacked, but some sharks might have attacked living mosasaurs, too.

A Ginsu (GIHN-soo) **shark attacks a mosasaur.**

Ferocious Fish

Sharks weren't the only killer fish in the Mesozoic ocean. Other ferocious fish lived beneath the waves as well. With razor-sharp fins, snouts, and teeth, these fish weren't very friendly! Read on to learn more about these fierce fish.

The X Factor

One of the largest fish was *Xiphactinus* (zye-FACK-tin-uhss) and this fish was no minnow! It grew to the size of a great white shark (about 15 feet or 5 m long), and had teeth as long as your middle finger! *Xiphactinus* is also called the "bulldog fish"—can you see why? This fish was a speedy swimmer that chased down its prey. It could open its mouth extra wide to gulp a meal down whole!

Xiphactinus

Q: Why did the *Xiphactinus* cross the ocean?

A: To get to the other *tide*!

***Xiphactinus* skeleton**

Protosphyraena

Follow Your Nose

Check out this Late Cretaceous fish called **Protosphyraena** (PRO-toe-sfie-RAY-nah). With its long, pointed snout, it looks a lot like a modern-day swordfish. Watch out for those side fins—they're super-sharp! *Protosphyraena* probably swam through a school of fish, used these fins to slash them, and then gobbled them up.

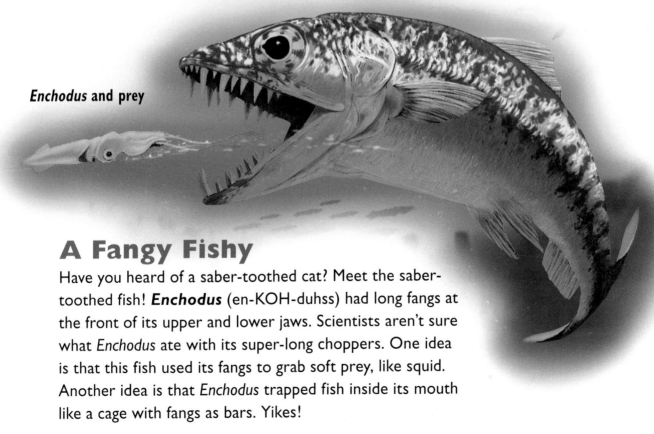

Enchodus **and prey**

A Fangy Fishy

Have you heard of a saber-toothed cat? Meet the saber-toothed fish! **Enchodus** (en-KOH-duhss) had long fangs at the front of its upper and lower jaws. Scientists aren't sure what *Enchodus* ate with its super-long choppers. One idea is that this fish used its fangs to grab soft prey, like squid. Another idea is that *Enchodus* trapped fish inside its mouth like a cage with fangs as bars. Yikes!

Shell Shocked

There was one really big reason that prehistoric sea turtles were *shell*-sational: they were BIG! Yup, some of the largest turtles that ever lived surfed the Mesozoic waves.

Big Guy

Check out **Archelon** (ARK-eh-lon), from the Late Cretaceous—the biggest turtle that ever lived! This turtle had a leathery shell like some modern-day sea turtles, but weighed as much as the meat-eating dino **Allosaurus** (AL-oh-SOR-uhss) and was 9–13 feet (3–4 m) wide. Though scientists don't know what giant *Archelon* ate, it had a very sharp, hooked beak that it could have used to eat jellyfish, seaweed, and maybe fish.

Archelon

DINO DATA

The largest *Archelon* ever discovered was found with its flippers folded and its head down. Scientists think this turtle died while sleeping on the seafloor.

Tasty Turtles

Protostega (PRO-toe-STEG-guh) was another giant prehistoric turtle, though not quite as big as *Archelon*. Even though these turtles were big, they weren't always safe from predators. Turtle bones have been found in the stomach of a mosasaur, and pieces of *Protostega* shell have been found with Ginsu shark teeth in them. There's even an *Archelon* fossil that's missing part of its back leg.

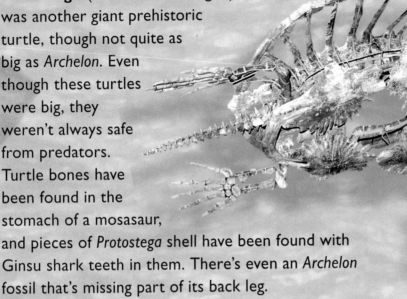

Protostega skeleton

Maybe a big predator had a snack attack!

Eggs-tra Effort

Unlike the prehistoric marine reptiles we've met so far, turtles laid eggs. Each year they swam to shore, which wasn't always a short trip. It could take days! Since these turtles' flippers were better on land than the paddles of other marine reptiles, they crawled onto land and dug nests to lay their eggs in, just like today's turtles do.

Turtle hatchling

Slow and Steady Wins the Race

Not all marine turtles were as big as *Archelon* and *Protostega*. Smaller turtles shared the water with these giants as well. Many were about the size of today's sea turtles. Just as ichthyosaurs, plesiosaurs, and mosasaurs were all extinct by the end of the Cretaceous, the giant turtles were gone by then as well. Although all the Mesozoic marine turtles became extinct, new ones evolved to take their place, and so sea turtles swim on today.

Incredible Invertebrates

An animal didn't need a mouthful of sharp teeth or a backbone to be a monster of the deep. Some **invertebrates** (in-VUR-tuh-brits) that lived in the Mesozoic ocean were pretty monstrous themselves, or at least monster-sized.

Blasting Off

Crinoids (KRY-noyds) and **blastoids** (BLASS-toyds) were two prehistoric invertebrates related to sea stars and sea urchins that lived on the Mesozoic seafloor. Both these animals had lots of bristly arms that caught tiny plants and animals floating in the water. Then the crinoids and blastoids swept these mini-meals into their mouths, which were in the center of their arms.

Crinoids and blastoids

Shell-Dwellers

Ammonites (AM-uhn-nites) were super-sized shell-dwellers that floated through the ocean. During the Late Cretaceous, some grew up to 13 feet (4 m) across! But don't let the shell fool you. Ammonites were actually related to octopuses and squid.

Fossil ammonites

DINO DATA

When ammonite shells were first discovered, people thought they were the fossils of curled-up snakes.

Super Squid

Jetting around in the water was the most monstrous of the invertebrates—a giant squid called **Tusoteuthis** (toos-oh-TOOTH-iss). It grew to be longer than three cars, and had a sharp beak in the center of its arms. Since a squid's soft body parts don't fossilize, the only thing that scientists find is a long, hard piece of shell, called a *pen*. Fossilized *Tusoteuthis* pens have been found with mosasaur bite marks on them, showing that these big squid may have tangled with some of the larger marine reptiles.

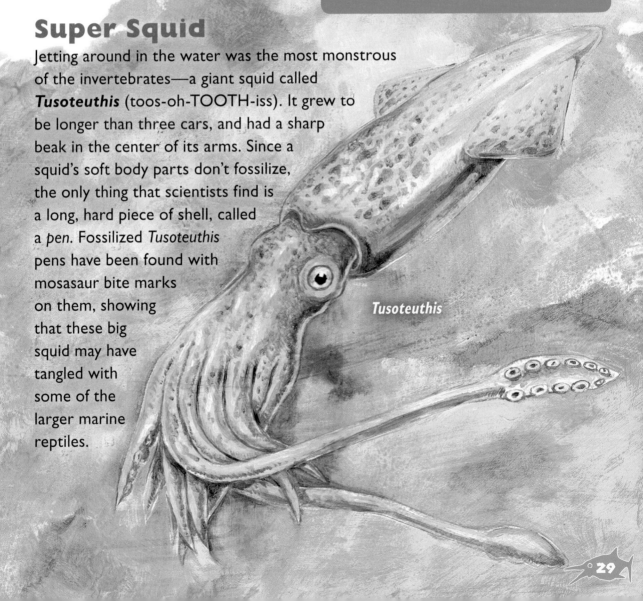

Tusoteuthis

PALEONTOLOGIST
ROBIN O'KEEFE

Meet Robin O'Keefe, a paleontologist who's been studying plesiosaurs for the last 10 years! Dr. O'Keefe studies how plesiosaurs' bodies evolved over time to help them live in water. We caught up with him to ask a few questions on these ocean giants.

Q How did you get interested in plesiosaurs?

A I became interested in plesiosaurs because I've always liked marine animals (like whales) and because I've always liked dinosaurs. Even though they're not dinos, plesiosaurs let me study large reptiles and marine animals at the same time.

Q How do you study how plesiosaurs swam?

A Scientists can study how extinct animals moved in two ways. The first way is to study modern-day animals with the same body shape. Scientists think that plesiosaurs swam like sea lions, so we can learn things by watching those animals. The other way to study movement is to look at the shape of an animal. We know that animals that have one kind of body shape can move in some ways, but can't move in other ways.

Q What's the strangest plesiosaur you've ever studied?

A The strangest plesiosaur I've ever studied is **Aristonectes** (uh-RIST-toh-NECK-tees) from the Late Cretaceous of Antarctica. *Aristonectes* had a long neck, big flippers, and a large head with a hoop-shaped jaw full of tiny teeth. We think that it gulped in water and fish like a pelican, and then strained the water out through its teeth like a flamingo.

Q What's your favorite plesiosaur?

A That's hard to say. *Kronosaurus* was the nastiest one, while *Elasmosaurus* had the longest neck. I think that a small, short-necked animal from the Cretaceous of Kansas and Nebraska called **Dolichorhynchops** (DOH-lick-oh-RINK-ops) is probably my favorite. It has a very beautiful skull and was fast and very graceful, with a long snout, like a dolphin in some ways, but with a very different way of swimming. I would like to have seen it alive!

Dr. O'Keefe in the field in Wyoming.

HENODUS

Say hello to *Henodus* (huh-NOH-dus)! Can you see why people say this weird-looking animal is like a cross between a walrus and a turtle? *Henodus* was covered with bony plates across its back and belly and used its broad, square snout to snuffle through soft mud for food. With only tiny teeth in the front of its mouth, *Henodus* probably ate soft-bodied invertebrates and shellfish. It used its two back teeth to crush shells and gobble up the tasty treats inside.

Henodus belonged to a strange group of slow-moving marine reptiles called **placodonts** (PLACK-oh-dahnts) that lived in the Triassic. Most placodonts were shellfish-eaters and some of them had bony armor for protection. While many placodonts lived in the ocean, *Henodus* lived in lagoons with less salty waters.

Maybe they should have called *Henodus* a wurtle!

Henodus

MORE DINO ADVENTURES COMING SOON!

Well, that's the end of our swim with sea monsters, and now it's time to come up for air! From ichthyosaurs to plesiosaurs to mosasaurs and more, we've gained a *deep* understanding of the creatures of the Mesozoic sea. We'll journey back to the Mesozoic soon for even more adventures. Till then, so long!

Ammonite